CW00549055

VENICE

TRAVEL GUIDE

2023

**The Ultimate Pocket guide to
Discover the Secrets,
Delights, and Hidden Gems
of Italy's Enchanting
Floating City.**

Clara Morgan

Copyrighted material

Copyright © 2023

Clara Morgan

All Rights Reserved. No part of this book may be reproduced, scanned, or distributed in any printed or electronic form without permission. Please do not participate in or encourage piracy of copyrighted materials in violation of the author's rights. Purchase only authorized editions.

This book is a work of nonfiction. The names, characters, places, and incidents are products of the author's imagination or have been used fictitiously and are not to be construed as real. Any resemblance to persons, living or dead, actual events, locales, or organizations is entirely coincidental.

Copyrighted material

MAP OF VENICE

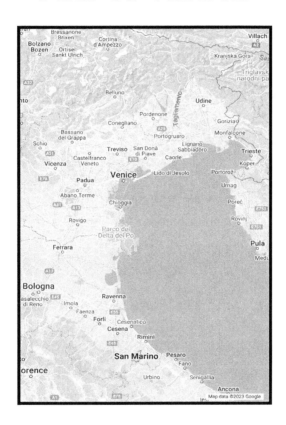

Copyrighted material

INTRODUCTION

HELLO AND WELCOME TO THE FLOATING CITY

Venice, popularly known as "The Floating City," is located in the Venetian Lagoon. This enthralling site is known for its ageless beauty, rich history, and romantic atmosphere.

Venice is unlike anywhere else, with canals replacing streets and gondolas gliding smoothly over the waterways, providing visitors with a one-of-a-kind and spectacular experience.

Venice is a true architectural marvel with its gorgeous palaces, exquisite bridges, and finely constructed buildings that display the city's historical riches and grandeur.

Copyrighted material

With its majestic church and soaring campanile, St. Mark's Square serves as Venice's showpiece and welcomes visitors to this extraordinary city.

Visiting Venice is like entering a live museum. The city is rich in art and culture, with world-class museums, churches embellished with exquisite murals, and hidden treasures around every corner.

Venice is a treasure mine of artistic and architectural delights, from Titian's and Tintoretto's works to the lavish interiors of the Doge's Palace.

Venice's unique network of canals is what truly distinguishes it. The lack of automobiles and roads generates a sense of calm and

Copyrighted material

allows guests to experience a means of transportation not found anywhere else.

As you float beneath stunning bridges and past charming waterfront buildings, a leisurely gondola ride around the canals provides a romantic and intimate perspective of the city.

Venice's gastronomic offerings also satisfy the senses. The city's cuisine is a celebration of fresh ingredients and local flavors, ranging from traditional Venetian cicchetti (little snacks) to exquisite seafood entrees.

Exploring local markets, such as the bustling Rialto Market, provides an opportunity to sample real Venetian cuisine. While Venice is undeniably a famous tourist destination, there are still hidden corners and quiet areas where

Copyrighted material

you may escape the crowds and explore the city from a more local perspective. Each neighborhood, from the artistic district of Dorsoduro to the historic streets of Castello, has its own distinct ambiance and treasures to explore.

For ages, Venice has inspired painters, writers, and dreamers, and it continues to enchant the hearts of all who visit. Venice promises a magical experience that will stay with you long after you've left, whether you're meandering through the narrow streets, admiring the dazzling reflections in the canals, or relishing a gelato while sitting by the water's edge.

So, prepare to be enchanted by Venice's charm, history, and enchantment as you start

Copyrighted material

on a journey through a city that has caught the mind of travelers for ages. Allow the beauty and romance of Venice to steal you away as you discover the riches that this amazing city has to offer.

VENICE BRIEF HISTORY

Venice, also known as the "Queen of the Adriatic" or the "Floating City," has a rich history dating back over 1,500 years. This amazing metropolis originated from the marshy islands of the Venetian Lagoon in the fifth century and flourished into a great maritime republic.

Venice was founded in 421 AD, according to mythology, when inhabitants from adjacent mainland towns sought sanctuary in the lagoon to escape invading barbarians. These

Copyrighted material

early inhabitants, known as Veneti, constructed their dwellings on wooden pilings pushed into the swampy land, laying the groundwork for the city's distinct architectural style.

As the Western Roman Empire fell apart, Venice had a period of relative autonomy and gradually grew into a prosperous trading city. Because of its strategic location at the crossroads of Europe and the Byzantine Empire, Venetian merchants were able to create profitable trading routes.

They amassed immense riches and influence through trading items such as spices, silk, and precious metals. During the Middle Ages and Renaissance, the Venetian Republic, also

Copyrighted material

known as the Serenissima, reached the pinnacle of its strength and influence.

The city-state adopted a republican system of administration, with the head magistrate being an elected doge. The Venetian fleet grew into a formidable force, allowing Venice to create colonies and extend its authority across the Adriatic and Mediterranean waters.

Venice's wealth during this time period can be linked to its strong maritime culture, skilled artisans, and thriving arts scene. The city became a haven for great artists and architects, who created masterpieces that may still be found in its palaces, churches, and public places. With the establishment of the world's first public library, the Biblioteca

Copyrighted material

Marciana, in the 16th century, the Venetian Republic also played an important role in preserving and sharing knowledge.

However, due to external pressures and shifting trade routes, Venice's political and economic supremacy began to wane in the 17th century. The discovery of new sea routes, as well as the growth of competing maritime powers, eroded Venice's trade monopoly. Furthermore, plague outbreaks and battles with surrounding powers weakened the city's position.

After centuries of supremacy, Venice surrendered to Napoleon Bonaparte's army in 1797 and became part of the Habsburg Empire. As Italy progressed toward nationhood, several political reforms and

Copyrighted material

unifications occurred. Venice was incorporated into the Kingdom of Italy in 1866.

Today, Venice is a symbol of its rich history and cultural richness. Its architectural marvels, including St. Mark's Basilica and the Doge's Palace, continue to astonish visitors from all over the world. The city's canals, gondolas, and exquisite bridges create a distinctively Venetian romantic and attractive ambiance.

You become part of a tradition that has defined the city's identity over generations as you explore the twisting lanes and experience the magic of Venice. Venice is a mesmerizing place that epitomizes the resilience, ingenuity, and attraction of the human spirit,

Copyrighted material

from its humble beginnings as a haven to its grandeur as a maritime empire.

LEARNING ABOUT VENETIAN CULTURE

Venice is a city with a rich and active cultural legacy, as well as beautiful architecture and picturesque canals. To properly understand the essence of Venice, it is necessary to immerse oneself in its distinct culture, customs, and way of life.

Carnival: The Carnival, a centuries-old celebration famed for its spectacular masks, costumes, and celebrations, is one of Venice's most memorable events. The city comes alive at this time with masquerade balls, street performances, and parades. Venetians and visitors alike can immerse themselves in the

Copyrighted material

mood of mystery, excess, and revelry during the Carnival.

Venetian Cuisine: Venetian cuisine is a delectable combination of flavors influenced by both the land and the sea. Seafood plays an important role in local cuisine, with popular dishes including sarde in saor (sweet and sour sardines) and risotto al nero di seppia (squid ink risotto). Don't miss out on cicchetti, little plates of delectable appetizers generally consumed with a glass of local wine at traditional bacari (wine bars).

Gondola Culture: The gondola is more than simply a form of transportation in Venice; it is also a symbol of the city. Gondoliers cross the small canals in classic striped shirts and straw caps, delivering a romantic and iconic

Copyrighted material

Venetian experience. Gondola rowing has been passed down through generations, and these exquisite boats have come to symbolize the city's attractiveness.

Murano, a small island near Venice, is famous for its centuries-old glassmaking tradition. Venetian glass is famous for its fine craftsmanship and vivid hues. Visit glass factories and experience the craftsmanship that goes into this delicate skill.

Venetian glassworks are valued globally, from elaborate chandeliers to delicate glass jewelry.

Voga Veneta: Voga Veneta, often known as Venetian rowing, is a centuries-old rowing style. Rowers stand facing forward, using a single oar to push their boats through the

Copyrighted material

water with grace and precision. Throughout the year, Voga Veneta races and regattas are staged to highlight the city's strong link to its nautical history.

Venice's architecture and art are a mix of styles that reflect its historical influences. The city's palaces, churches, and public structures contain Byzantine, Gothic, and Renaissance characteristics. During the Renaissance, the Venetian art scene flourished, with renowned artists such as Titian, Tintoretto, and Veronese leaving a legacy of masterpieces that can still be seen in museums and galleries.

Local Dialect: Venetian, also known as Veneziano, is still spoken by some residents and is considered a unique regional language.

Copyrighted material

Despite the fact that Italian is the official language, hearing Venetians speak in their own dialect gives a genuine touch to the cultural experience.

By immersing yourself in Venetian culture, you will obtain a better understanding of the city's history and the traditions that have defined its identity. To truly appreciate the unique cultural tapestry that makes this floating city so beautiful, immerse yourself in the festivals, sample the local food, discover the art scene, and interact with the kind and hospitable people of Venice.

Copyrighted material

MAKING TRAVEL PLANS

Copyrighted material

CHAPTER 1

MAKING TRAVEL PLANS

The best time to visit Venice is determined largely by your choices and the experiences you seek. To help you make an informed selection, below is a breakdown of the different seasons in Venice:

Spring (March to May): Compared to the summer months, spring in Venice has milder weather and fewer visitors. It's a fantastic time to visit the city's attractions while enjoying the nice weather. However, keep in mind that April might still be a busy month due to the Easter holiday.

Summer (June to August): Summer is the busiest tourist season in Venice, with high

Copyrighted material

visitor numbers and mild temperatures. The city can become congested, particularly around popular landmarks. Summer, on the other hand, provides extended daylight hours, allowing you to make the most of your visit. To avoid the busiest times, go exploring early in the morning or late in the evening.

Autumn (September to November): Autumn is widely regarded as one of the greatest times to visit Venice. The weather stays beautiful, and crowds begin to drop out in comparison to the summer.

September, in particular, provides a pleasant mix of warm days and mild evenings, making it a perfect month for sightseeing and outdoor activities. The months of October and November bring lower temperatures, but you

Copyrighted material

may still experience Venice's charm with fewer tourists.

Winter (December to February): Venice in winter offers a one-of-a-kind experience with fewer tourists and a more relaxed atmosphere. However, keep in mind that the city has colder temperatures, occasional fog, and a higher possibility of rain.

Winter might be a fantastic season to visit Venice if you don't mind the cooler weather and want to experience the magical ambiance without the crowds. Furthermore, Venice's Carnival, which is normally held in February, is a major highlight of the winter season.

It's also worth thinking about the Acqua Alta phenomenon, which occurs when high tides flood portions of Venice.

Copyrighted material

These occurrences are more common throughout the winter months, especially from October to December. While they might be difficult to navigate, they also offer a unique perspective on the city's relationship with water and can be intriguing to see.

Consider the benefits and drawbacks of each season to plan a journey that matches your interests and intended experiences in the gorgeous "Floating City."

LIST OF ESSENTIALS TO PACK

Here's a concise list of essentials to pack when traveling to Venice:

1. Passport and travel documents
2. Lightweight clothing for warm weather
3. Comfortable walking shoes
4. Sunscreen and a hat for sun protection

Copyrighted material

5. Camera or smartphone for capturing the beautiful sights

6. Umbrella or raincoat for unpredictable weather

7. Adapter and charger for electronic devices

8. Small backpack or bag for daily use

9. Insect repellent (especially during warmer months)

10. Basic toiletries and any necessary medications.

Remember to also check the weather forecast before you go, so you can pack accordingly.

VISA REQUIREMENTS AND TRAVEL REQUIREMENTS

It's critical to understand the visa and travel requirements for entering Italy before

Copyrighted material

planning a trip to Venice. Consider the following crucial points:

<u>Validity of Passport</u>: Make sure your passport is valid for at least six months beyond your planned stay in Italy. Most countries' citizens are subject to this regulation.

<u>Visa Requirements</u>: Italy is a member of the Schengen Area, which allows people to travel between selected European nations without needing to obtain separate visas for each.If you are a Schengen Area citizen, you can enter Italy without a visa for up to 90 days within a 180-day period.

This covers numerous European countries, as well as the United States, Canada, Australia, and New Zealand. However, depending on your nationality, you should examine the

Copyrighted material

exact visa requirements since certain countries may have different accords or require visas for access.

Visa-Free Travel: If you are a citizen of a country with a visa-free travel agreement with the Schengen Area, you can enter Italy without a visa and remain for up to 90 days within a 180-day period. This is common for short-term tourism; business travels, or family visits. Before going, it is critical to confirm the visa exemption laws for your country of citizenship.

If you are a citizen of a country that does not have a visa-free travel agreement with the Schengen Area, you must apply for a Schengen Visa before your trip. This includes

Copyrighted material

citizens of China, India, Russia, and many more countries.

For further information on the visa application process, required documents, and processing periods, contact the nearest Italian embassy or consulate in your home country.

Travel Insurance: Although not required for entrance, having travel insurance that covers medical expenditures and probable trip disruptions during your stay in Italy is highly advised. This ensures that you are appropriately protected in the event of an unforeseen event.

Travel Requirements for COVID-19: Due to the current COVID-19 epidemic, travel requirements, and limitations may vary. Check the Italian Ministry of Foreign Affairs

Copyrighted material

official website or contact your local embassy or consulate for the most recent updates on COVID-19 travel regulations, including any testing or vaccine requirements, quarantine measures, and travel advisories. Remember to plan and prepare for your trip ahead of time, ensuring that you have the appropriate travel documents and meet all applicable standards.

Checking official government websites and obtaining advice from relevant authorities will offer you the most accurate and up-to-date information for your individual situation.

VENICE TRANSPORTATION OPTIONS

Venice, sometimes known as the "Floating City," has a unique transportation system due

Copyrighted material

to its network of canals and lack of car streets. Here are the main modes of transportation available in Venice:

<u>Vaporettos (Water Buses):</u> Vaporettos are water buses that are the primary means of public transit in Venice. They run on numerous routes that connect various parts of the city and adjacent islands. Vaporettos are a cheap and convenient method to get around Venice, and they often run throughout the day. Tickets are available at ticket booths and automated devices at Vaporetto stops. It is recommended that you validate your ticket upon boarding.

<u>Water Taxis:</u> Water taxis are private boats that offer a more customized and speedier means of transportation in Venice.

Copyrighted material

They cost more than Vaporettos but provide the convenience of direct routes and customizable itineraries. Water taxis can be requested at designated taxi stations or through a hotel or private service.

Gondolas: Gondolas are a characteristic Venice emblem, especially linked with romantic canal cruises. While gondolas are mostly utilized for tourism, they may be a fun and unique method to explore the city. Gondolas are normally operated by certified gondoliers and can be hired throughout Venice. It is critical to pre-arrange the price and duration of the ride.

Walking: Because Venice is a pedestrian-friendly city, walking is a common and delightful mode of

Copyrighted material

transportation. The compact nature of the city allows for convenient exploration on foot, particularly in the center sections. Walking through Venice's small streets, across lovely bridges, and uncovering hidden gems is a delightful experience.

<u>Traghetti</u>: Traghetti are enormous gondola-like boats that ferry passengers across the Grand Canal at various points. They provide a faster alternative to utilizing the standard bridges to traverse the canal.

Traghetti rides are often brief and stand-up affairs, with passengers just standing while crossing. The stops for the Traghetti are prominently marked, and tickets can be purchased straight on board.

Copyrighted material

<u>Private Boats:</u> For special occasions or bespoke experiences, Venice provides a variety of private boat services, including water limos and water shuttles. These alternatives offer a premium and exclusive way to experience Venice and its environs.

It is vital to remember that there are no cars or bicycles within the old core of Venice due to the lack of motor highways. Porters or luggage delivery services can transfer luggage, particularly from train stations or authorized drop-off sites.

Each mode of transportation in Venice provides a distinct experience, and your choice will be determined by your interests, budget, and itinerary.

Copyrighted material

Whether you choose vaporettos for their convenience, gondolas for their romantic beauty, or water taxis for their speed, navigating Venice's picturesque canals is guaranteed to be an unforgettable part of your vacation.

VENICE ACCOMMODATION

Venice has a wide choice of hotel alternatives to suit all tastes and budgets. There is something for every traveler, from luxurious hotels with canal views to modest bed and breakfasts nestled away in peaceful corners. Here are some examples of frequent types of accommodation in Venice:

Hotels: Hotels in Venice range from budget-friendly options to magnificent five-star places.

Copyrighted material

Hotels can be found throughout the city, including the core regions of San Marco and Cannaregio, as well as on the islands of Murano and Lido. Hotels in Venice frequently have distinctive architectural elements and offer a variety of amenities such as restaurants, bars, and concierge services.

Bed and Breakfasts (B&Bs): B&Bs provide a more intimate and homey setting. They are often smaller in size and are frequently operated by local families. B&Bs may be located all across Venice, offering guests a comfortable and individualized experience. Some bed and breakfasts include breakfast, while others provide cooking facilities for visitors to prepare their own meals.

Copyrighted material

<u>Guesthouses and Inns:</u> Guesthouses and inns are smaller accommodations that are less expensive than hotels. They frequently offer fewer rooms but, nevertheless, provide comfortable and convenient accommodations. Guesthouses are typically family-run and provide a more personalized experience, whereas inns may have additional amenities such as on-site restaurants or common areas.

<u>Apartments and Vacation Rentals:</u> For travelers who desire greater space and the freedom of self-catering, renting an apartment or vacation rental is a popular alternative. In Venice, you may discover apartments ranging from small studios to larger units perfect for families or groups.

Copyrighted material

Vacation rentals allow you to experience Venice like a local, with the added convenience of kitchens and living areas.

Boutique & Design Hotels: Venice features a number of boutique and design hotels for visitors looking for a distinctive and stylish experience. These lodgings frequently offer contemporary or themed designs that showcase modern aesthetics while preserving the city's historic charm.

Boutique hotels are often smaller in size and provide more customized service. Consider variables such as location, budget, amenities, and the type of experience you seek when booking your Venice accommodations. Staying in downtown Venice neighborhoods such as San Marco or Dorsoduro provides convenient access

Copyrighted material

to key attractions, while hotels in quieter regions can give a more serene respite. It's best to reserve your accommodations ahead of time, especially during peak tourist season or if you have specific preferences.

Regardless of the type of accommodation you pick, staying in Venice allows you to immerse yourself in the city's distinct ambiance and charm, providing an unforgettable experience in this enthralling "Floating City."

FOOD AND WINE EXPERIENCES IN VENETIAN CUISINE

Venetian cuisine is a culinary treat that represents the city of Venice's distinct culture, history, and geography.

Venice, located in the Veneto region of Italy, is surrounded by water and inspired by both Italian and Mediterranean cuisines, resulting

Copyrighted material

in a distinct culinary legacy enjoyed by both locals and visitors.

Given the city's location on the Adriatic Sea, seafood plays an important role in Venetian cuisine. Menus notably highlight fresh fish such as bream, sea bass, sardines, and cuttlefish. One classic dish is "Risotto al nero di seppia," a rich and savory black squid ink risotto that highlights the region's maritime origins.

Another seafood specialty is "Fritto misto," a delectable combination of fried shellfish that frequently includes shrimp, calamari, and small fish.

Venice is also known for its "Cicchetti," which are small plates of excellent bite-sized nibbles that are generally consumed with a

Copyrighted material

glass of local wine. These can range from basic bruschetta with fresh tomatoes and basil to more complicated dishes like marinated seafood, fried polenta, or the creamy codfish spread known as "Baccalà Mantecato."

Cicchetti bars are popular meeting places for residents, offering a lively and communal dining experience.When it comes to pasta, Venetian food has its own distinct style.

"Bigoli" is a thick, long pasta that is usually served with a savory sauce of onions, anchovies, and sardines. "Pasta e Fagioli," a rich and soothing soup with pasta and beans in a delicious broth, is another classic pasta meal. Venetian cuisine also includes delightful options for meat lovers. The classic

Copyrighted material

meal "Fegato alla Veneziana" is calf's liver sautéed with onions, creating a rich and savory mixture. "Risi e Bisi" is a traditional Venetian risotto cooked with fresh peas and pancetta that highlights the characteristics of the region.

No trip to Venice would be complete without indulging in some sweet delicacies. "Tiramisu" is a favorite regional delicacy made of layers of coffee-soaked ladyfingers and creamy mascarpone cheese. "Fritole" are miniature fried doughnuts that are usually eaten during the Carnival season and are often filled with raisins, pine nuts, or candied fruit. Venice offers a variety of local wines to complement these delectable dishes,

Copyrighted material

including the famed sparkling wine "Prosecco" and the crisp white wine "Soave." For those looking for a one-of-a-kind digestif, the city is well-known for its "Spritz," a delightful cocktail mixed with Aperol or Campari, sparkling water, and a splash of white wine or Prosecco.

Venetian cuisine is a celebration of fresh ingredients, robust flavors, and the city's culinary traditions. It encourages you to enjoy the flavors of the sea, the bounty of the land, and the passion of its people. Exploring Venice's numerous gastronomic options is a crucial aspect of immersing oneself in this magnificent city's colorful and tasty culture.

Copyrighted material

CHAPTER 2

VENICE NEIGHBORHOOD EXPLORATION

SAN MARCO: THE HEART OF VENICE

San Marco is one of Venice's most recognizable and historically significant neighborhoods. It is a busy and bustling district that shows the city's grandeur and architectural magnificence and is named after St. Mark's Square (Piazza San Marco).

St. Mark's Square, located in the center of San Marco, is a stunning open space surrounded by amazing landmarks. St. Mark's Basilica is the main attraction, an

Copyrighted material

awe-inspiring basilica known for its Byzantine architecture, beautiful mosaics, and elaborate embellishments. Visitors can marvel at the magnificent interior and appreciate the basilica's cherished artifacts, notably the Pala d'Oro, an amazing golden altarpiece.

Adjacent to the church lies the spectacular Doge's Palace, a Gothic masterpiece that served as the house and seat of power for the Doge of Venice.

Exploring the palace's exquisite apartments and spectacular halls, as well as crossing the famed Bridge of Sighs that connects the palace to the prisons, provides an intriguing peek into the city's rich history.

Copyrighted material

The Campanile di San Marco, a towering bell tower in the square, provides panoramic views of Venice. Ascending to the summit provides visitors with stunning views of the city's roofs, canals, and surrounding lagoon.

San Marco is home to upmarket shops, exquisite boutiques, and renowned cafes, in addition to its spectacular landmarks. It is ideal for luxury shopping, discovering traditional Venetian crafts, and enjoying a coffee or delectable pastry at ancient places such as Caffè Florian or Caffè Quadri.

Visitors can immerse themselves in the magnificence and charm of Venice by exploring San Marco. The architectural marvels, cultural attractions, and energetic

Copyrighted material

ambiance of the neighborhood make for a unique experience. Despite its popularity, San Marco's appeal continues to attract travelers, making it a must-see location for anybody looking to uncover the true spirit of Venice.

DORSODURO: CULTURE AND ART

Dorsoduro, a bustling area in Venice, Italy, combines art, culture, and Venetian charm. Dorsoduro, located on the Grand Canal's southern bank, is a vibrant neighborhood famed for its creative institutions, gorgeous canals, and bustling atmosphere. The Peggy Guggenheim Collection, situated in the former home of the famed art collector Peggy Guggenheim, is one of Dorsoduro's

Copyrighted material

highlights. This modern art museum houses an impressive collection of twentieth-century works by artists such as Picasso, Pollock, and Dal. The museum's beautiful garden and canal view make it a relaxing and fascinating location to visit.

The Gallerie dell'Accademia is another important cultural institution in Dorsoduro. This museum, housed in the ancient Scuola Grande di Santa Maria della Carità, displays a large collection of Venetian art from the 14th to the 18th century.

Visitors can appreciate masterpieces by renowned artists such as Titian, Tintoretto, and Veronese, which provide a profound insight into Venice's cultural past.

Copyrighted material

Dorsoduro also houses Ca' Foscari University, which attracts a vibrant student population that contributes to the neighborhood's energetic and creative atmosphere. Dorsoduro has a youthful spirit because of the presence of students, and the area is studded with pleasant cafes, fashionable pubs, and bohemian hangouts.

Exploring Dorsoduro's canals and small lanes is a lovely experience. In comparison to other districts of Venice, the neighborhood features magnificent bridges, charming squares, and less busy paths, providing a quieter and more authentic feel.

Exploring the maze lanes and discovering hidden jewels, local artisan shops, and small galleries is an experience in and of itself.

Copyrighted material

Dorsoduro's distinct personality and cultural amenities make it a favorite among art lovers, students, and those looking for a livelier and less touristy side of Venice. Dorsoduro is an enticing district for visitors wishing to immerse themselves in the city's cultural and intellectual heart, thanks to its combination of world-class museums, artistic legacy, and calm attitude.

CANNAREGIO: TRADITIONAL VENETIAN CHARM

Cannaregio, a diverse and bustling district in Venice, Italy, provides a distinct combination of history, local charm, and hidden discoveries. It is one of Venice's largest and most authentic districts, located in the city's northern outskirts.

Copyrighted material

Cannaregio is famous for its peaceful canals, scenic bridges, and narrow lanes that evoke an old-world elegance. Unlike the crowded tourist regions, this neighborhood offers a more residential and local experience, allowing visitors to immerse themselves in Venetian daily life.

The Jewish Ghetto, the oldest Jewish Ghetto in Europe, is one of Cannaregio's most prominent landmarks. The area is home to synagogues, museums, and kosher eateries due to its rich history and cultural significance.

Visitors can learn about the lively Jewish community that has shaped the neighborhood's identity by exploring the Jewish Ghetto.

Copyrighted material

The Strada Nova, a busy boulevard that runs through Cannaregio, is dotted with shops, boutiques, cafes, and traditional Cannaregio eateries. It gives a lovely shopping and dining experience away from the more touristic districts, as well as a view into the daily lives of people as they go about their business.

Another attraction of Cannaregio is the Fondamenta della Misericordia, a lovely canal-side promenade. This picturesque waterfront district is peppered with classic Venetian pubs known as "bacari," where you may try local cicchetti (small nibbles) and sip a bottle of wine. It's a popular hangout for locals and provides a relaxing and authentic Venetian vibe.

Copyrighted material

Cannaregio also has some lovely churches worth visiting, like the Church of Madonna dell'Orto and the Church of San Giobbe. These lesser-known churches frequently feature beautiful artworks and offer a calm reprieve from the crowds.

You'll come across beautiful squares, hidden courtyards, and neighborhood markets as you walk through Cannaregio's twisting lanes. In comparison to the city's central regions, the neighborhood has a quieter, more laid-back atmosphere, allowing tourists to appreciate the slower pace of life and discover hidden gems around every corner.

Cannaregio offers a welcome respite from the tourist crowds and a genuine Venetian experience.

Copyrighted material

Its local charm, historical monuments, and welcoming attitude make it an enchanting district to explore and an ideal alternative for anyone looking for an off-the-beaten-path trip in Venice.

CASTELLO: HISTORICAL RELICS

Castello, a neighborhood in the eastern section of Venice, blends local beauty, historical value, and a quiet atmosphere. It spans from the Arsenale to the city's eastern tip and provides a look into Venice's real side.

Castello is well-known for its authentic Venetian architecture, tiny lanes, and peaceful waterways.

Copyrighted material

It has a more residential vibe than the bustling tourist zones, giving tourists a taste of regular Venetian life.

This neighborhood is popular among locals and visitors looking for a more tranquil side of Venice. The Arsenale, a historic shipyard and naval station that played an important role in Venice's maritime strength during the Middle Ages, is one of the principal attractions of Castello. Although most of the region is inaccessible to the public, glimpses of the amazing structures can be seen from the outside.

The Arsenale also hosts the Venice Biennale, an internationally recognized art show held every two years. Castello also has public gardens known as Giardini della Biennale.

Copyrighted material

These gardens provide a pleasant respite from the hectic city streets and a spot to rest, stroll lazily or enjoy a picnic. During the Venice Biennale, the gardens are attractively groomed and house a variety of art exhibits and pavilions.

Several important churches may be found in Castello, including the Church of San Zaccaria and the Church of San Francesco della Vigna. These churches have beautiful architectural elements and noteworthy artworks by well-known Venetian artists.

Exploring these cathedrals enables tourists to appreciate Venice's rich religious and cultural legacy. Castello has picturesque squares, small markets, and historic Venetian osterias and trattorias, where you may experience true

Copyrighted material

Venetian cuisine. Away from the tourist traps, the neighborhood offers a chance to enjoy a more real dining experience. Castello's location on Venice's eastern outskirts also provides spectacular waterfront views and the opportunity to explore the city's less congested districts.

You can take a walk along the fondamenta (quayside) and admire the tranquil waterways and gorgeous bridges. Castello is a serene hideaway for anyone looking for a quieter and more local experience in Venice.

Its historic sites, classic architecture, and quiet ambiance combine to form a lovely area that exhibits the city's distinct character and offers a look into Venetian daily life.

Copyrighted material

SANTA CROCE: HIDDEN GEMS

Santa Croce, located in the western section of Venice, is a charming area with a combination of historical landmarks, local life, and scenic waterways. Here's what to expect when visiting Santa Croce:

Views of the Grand Canal: Santa Croce is located on the Grand Canal, one of Venice's most famous waterways. You'll be treated to stunning views of passing gondolas, traditional Venetian palaces, and active activity on the water as you stroll along the canal-side promenades and bridges. It's an ideal location for admiring Venice's beauty and taking great images.

Copyrighted material

San Giacomo dell'Orio: This charming square serves as the heart of Santa Croce and provides a calm retreat from the city's busier areas. The square is centered on San Giacomo dell'Orio Church, a stunning specimen of Venetian Gothic architecture.

In this hidden gem of a square, take a moment to absorb the gorgeous surroundings and soak up the local ambiance.

The Scuola Grande di San Rocco, located in Santa Croce, is a majestic structure filled with masterpieces by Tintoretto, one of Venice's most famous painters. The interior is richly decorated with exquisite murals depicting biblical scenes, offering guests an enthralling artistic experience.

Copyrighted material

Local Markets and Delis: There are various local markets and delis in Santa Croce where you may sample real Venetian cuisine. Rialto Market, located on the boundary of Santa Croce and San Polo, sells fresh produce, fish, and regional delicacies. It's the ideal place to immerse yourself in Venice's bustling food culture and savor delectable snacks.

The Scalzi Bridge, which connects Santa Croce to the Cannaregio district, is an iconic landmark. This magnificent stone bridge provides a lovely crossing across the Grand Canal and offers breathtaking views of the surrounding area. It's a great place to see the architecture and take panoramic shots of Venice.

Copyrighted material

Fondaco dei Turchi: The Fondaco dei Turchi is a historic edifice near the Scalzi Bridge that today houses the Museum of Natural History. The museum displays fossils, minerals, and archaeological objects, providing insights into the natural history of Venice and the surrounding region.

Santa Croce offers a more peaceful and authentic experience in Venice. It offers a beautiful blend of local life and cultural attractions, with its charming squares, picturesque canals, and historical sites. Exploring Santa Croce allows you to experience Venice's own personality while also discovering hidden treasures in this charming district.

Copyrighted material

Copyrighted material

CHAPTER 3

LANDMARKS AND TOP ATTRACTIONS

THE BASILICA AND ST. MARK'S SQUARE

St. Mark's Square, also known as Piazza San Marco, is the beating heart of Venice, Italy. This landmark plaza is a stunning public place that has served as the city's political, religious, and social hub for centuries. St. Mark's Square, surrounded by architectural marvels and ornamented with historical significance, is a tribute to Venice's grandeur and majesty.

Copyrighted material

The majestic St. Mark's Basilica, one of the world's most recognized specimens of Byzantine architecture, is at the center of the square. This magnificent masterwork bears witness to Venice's rich history and cultural heritage. The basilica is a marvel to behold, with its beautiful mosaics, golden domes, and magnificent exterior.

St. Mark's Basilica's interior is similarly stunning. When you enter, you'll be enveloped in a world of Byzantine artistry and splendor. Admire the golden mosaics on the walls and ceilings, which represent religious images and elaborate designs. Admire the exquisite marble floors, which are covered with lovely designs and themes.

Copyrighted material

Another must-see is the Pala d'Oro, a stunning altarpiece studded with expensive stones and delicate enamelwork. The rising Campanile di San Marco, a bell tower next to the basilica, offers panoramic views of Venice from its observation deck.

Ascend to the top for a panoramic view of the city, its canals, and the surrounding lagoon. The campanile is an ideal location for taking great images and truly appreciating Venice's magnificence.

The Doge's Palace, an architectural marvel that historically served as the residence of the Doge, the ultimate power of the Venetian Republic, is also located in St. Mark's Square. This magnificent castle features Venetian Gothic architecture, a beautiful

Copyrighted material

façade, exquisite arches, and intricate sculptures. Inside, you can stroll among the opulent apartments, examine great works of art, and cross the famed Bridge of Sighs, which connects the palace to the neighboring prison.

The square itself is a hive of activity, with outdoor cafes, beautiful boutiques, and street entertainers contributing to the lively atmosphere. Take a seat at a café, sip a traditional Venetian coffee, and observe the world go by as locals and visitors alike congregate in this historic meeting point.

St. Mark's Square and Basilica represent the grandeur and cultural significance of Venice. They provide witness to the city's illustrious history, architectural grandeur, and creative

Copyrighted material

legacy. A visit to this amazing piazza is a must for any Venetian trip, allowing you to immerse yourself in the beauty and charm of this extraordinary city.

THE DOGE PALACE AND THE BRIDGE OF SIGHS

The Doge's Palace in Venice's St. Mark's Square is a remarkable testimony to the city's rich history and architectural magnificence.

For centuries, this magnificent palace was the residence of the Doge, the supreme power of the Venetian Republic, and the center of government.

Today, it represents Venice's strength, richness, and creative prowess. The Doge's Palace features outstanding Venetian Gothic architecture, with graceful arches, delicate

Copyrighted material

tracery, and rich statues adorning its complicated front. You'll be impressed by the palace's grand appearance as you approach it, a towering monument that embodies Venice's reputation as a maritime empire.

Stepping inside the Doge's Palace transports you back in time. The interior design is a work of art, with sumptuous apartments decorated with fine artworks, elaborate paintings, and gilded ornaments. Explore the majestic rooms, such as the Sala del Maggior Consiglio, where the Great Council met, and the Doge's Apartments, which provide an insight into the ruling Doge's lavish lifestyle. The Bridge of Sighs is a well-known feature of the Doge's Palace.

Copyrighted material

This enclosed bridge, which connects the palace to the adjacent prison, has a fascinating history and generates a sense of suspense. Lord Byron gave the bridge the name "Bridge of Sighs" because it was thought that convicts would sigh as they had their final glimpse of the outside world before entering the jail. The bridge is still a famous tourist destination today, and its stone arches and artistic ornamentation continue to captivate visitors.

Exploring the Doge's Palace and crossing the Bridge of Sighs immerses you in Venice's rich tapestry of history. You'll learn about the city's political and legal processes, as well as admire Venetian artists' aesthetic triumphs.

Copyrighted material

The palace's complex layout, secret tunnels, and hidden chambers add to the sense of mystery and adventure. Aside from its historical significance, the Doge's Palace has stunning views of the lagoon, St. Mark's Square, and the surrounding metropolis. Ascend to the rooftop terraces, and you'll be rewarded with magnificent views of Venice's beauty and distinctiveness.

A visit to the Doge's Palace and the Bridge of Sighs takes you deep into Venetian history and culture. It allows you to tread in the footsteps of historical rulers, appreciate spectacular architecture, and learn about the city's traditions and legends. Prepare to be charmed by the beauty and intrigue that these magnificent landmarks have to offer.

Copyrighted material

THE RIALTO BRIDGE AND THE GRAND CANAL

The Rialto Bridge and the Grand Canal are two prominent sights in Venice, Italy, that capture the soul of the city. They are must-see sights for any tourist as emblems of the city's rich history, architectural prowess, and dynamic culture.

One of Venice's most recognized and treasured sights is the Rialto Bridge, which spans the Grand Canal. This architectural gem joins the San Marco and San Polo districts, acting as an important crossing point and a hub of activity. The bridge has a long history that dates back to the 16th century, and its distinctive design includes a

Copyrighted material

central portico lined with businesses, providing a lively and bustling environment.

The Rialto Bridge is an adventure in and of itself. Take a moment to absorb the stunning views of the Grand Canal as you cross the bridge. Gondolas and vaporettos (water buses) float smoothly along the waterway, which is lined with palaces and historic structures. The bridge provides a vantage point from which to view Venice's lively energy and marine character.

The Grand Canal, Venice's major waterway, is a gleaming ribbon that snakes its way through the city's heart. This historic waterway is known as the "most beautiful street in the world" and is a monument to Venice's architectural magnificence.

Copyrighted material

The Grand Canal, which is lined with palaces, churches, and noble mansions, exhibits the city's rich history as well as the architectural styles of several centuries.

Boating through the Grand Canal is a magical experience. To gently traverse the canal's waters, take a vaporetto or a romantic gondola ride. You'll pass beneath magnificent bridges and see the stunning facades of grand palaces like Ca' d'Oro and Palazzo Grassi as you travel.

The Grand Canal's ever-changing landscapes and stunning surroundings provide unlimited photo opportunities as well as an insight into the Venetian way of life.

Copyrighted material

The Rialto Bridge and the Grand Canal are not just architectural marvels, but they also symbolize the spirit of commerce and cultural interchange that has distinguished Venice throughout history.

They are reminders of Venice's maritime strength as well as its significance as a commercial and creative innovation center. Visiting the Rialto Bridge and the Grand Canal allows you to immerse yourself in Venice's unique ambiance.

It's a chance to see the city's stunning beauty, architectural majesty, and the eternal charm of its waterways. Whether you're crossing the bridge or cruising down the canal, the experience will leave an everlasting imprint,

Copyrighted material

highlighting Venice's enchantment and magnificence.

THE GALLERIE DELL'ACCADEMIA

The Gallerie dell'Accademia is a prominent art museum in Venice, Italy's Dorsoduro area. It is one of the city's most important cultural institutions, featuring an extraordinary collection of Venetian art dating from the 14th to the 18th centuries.

A visit to this museum provides an enthralling tour through the evolution of Venetian art and a better knowledge of the city's rich cultural legacy. The museum is housed in the former Scuola della Carità, which emanates history and grandeur.

Copyrighted material

Visitors are greeted upon entry by a broad collection of masterpieces showcasing the talents of prominent Venetian artists. Paintings, sculptures, and drawings are among the mediums represented in the exhibition.

The Gallerie dell'Accademia's collection of Venetian Renaissance art is one of its centerpieces. Masterworks by Giovanni Bellini, Titian, Veronese, and Tintoretto are on display for visitors to admire.

The brilliant colors, complex details, and deft brushwork in these paintings attest to the artistic genius that flourished in Venice during this time period.

Copyrighted material

The museum also has a large collection of religious art, which includes altarpieces, religious sculptures, and devotional objects. These works provide insights into the theological and cultural contexts in which they were created, as well as a view into Venice's spiritual life over the centuries.

The Gallerie dell'Accademia, in addition to its permanent collection, organizes temporary exhibitions that explore diverse themes and artistic movements. These exhibitions allow visitors to delve deeper into specific parts of Venetian art while also providing a new perspective on the city's cultural past.

A visit to the Gallerie dell'Accademia is an opportunity to reflect on the artistry and creativity that have formed Venice.

Copyrighted material

The museum offers a tranquil haven away from the busy canals, allowing visitors to immerse themselves in the beauty and contemplation of art. The beautifully selected displays and informative labeling add to the experience by providing context and background information about the artworks.

A visit to the Gallerie dell'Accademia is a must during your vacation to Venice, whether you are an art connoisseur or simply admire the beauty of visual expression. It provides an exceptional opportunity to see the growth of Venetian art and gain a deeper understanding of this amazing city's cultural legacy.

Copyrighted material

COLLECTION OF PEGGY GUGGENHEIM

The Peggy Guggenheim Collection is a magnificent art museum located on Venice's Grand Canal. The museum displays the personal collection of Peggy Guggenheim, a prominent art patron, and collector, and is housed in the mansion Venier dei Leoni, a former unfinished mansion.

A visit to this museum is an immersive trip through modern and contemporary art, exhibiting works by some of the twentieth century's most prominent painters.

The Peggy Guggenheim Collection represents a diverse spectrum of artistic trends and genres, including Cubism, Surrealism, Abstract Expressionism, and

Copyrighted material

others. It includes works by well-known painters like Pablo Picasso, Jackson Pollock, Wassily Kandinsky, Salvador Dal, and many more. The collection, which includes everything from classic paintings to interesting sculptures, provides a complete overview of modern art and its revolutionary impact.

The museum is a work of art in and of itself, with its exquisite and small setting providing a great backdrop for the exhibits. As you walk through the galleries, you'll come across a plethora of classics that excite thinking, elicit passion, and defy conventional aesthetic boundaries.

Peggy Guggenheim's acute eye for revolutionary artists and her commitment to

Copyrighted material

encouraging creative and daring art movements are reflected in the collection. Aside from the permanent collection, the museum frequently presents temporary exhibitions, which improve the visitor's experience by introducing different views and themes. These exhibitions reflect the changing nature of modern art and provide budding artists with a chance to show off their skills.

The picturesque garden overlooking the Grand Canal is one of the centerpieces of the Peggy Guggenheim Collection. This calm outdoor spot comprises sculptures by artists such as Marino Marini and serves as a peaceful haven in the heart of the metropolis. Visitors can unwind, think, and admire the

Copyrighted material

beautiful blend of art and environment. The Peggy Guggenheim Collection is not only a treasure trove of modern and contemporary art, but it also bears witness to Peggy Guggenheim's enduring influence on the art world. Her love of art and commitment to supporting artists and artistic trends continue to inspire both visitors and artists.

A visit to the Peggy Guggenheim Collection provides a profound and engaging experience for art lovers and casual tourists alike, allowing them to engage with the transforming power of art. It's a celebration of creativity, invention, and the lasting legacy of one amazing woman's vision.

Copyrighted material

A couple on masks under the colonnade of St Mark's Square during the Venice Carnival .

Copyrighted material

CHAPTER 4

FESTIVALS AND SPECIAL EVENTS

VENICE CARNIVAL: A MAGICAL CELEBRATION

The Venice Carnival is a world-famous carnival that captures the imagination and soul of this magical city. The Carnival, which dates back centuries, has become linked with vivid costumes, extravagant masks, and a sense of mystery and intrigue. It is a season when Venice comes alive with celebrations, attracting tourists from all over the world to experience its distinct blend of history, culture, and festivity.

Copyrighted material

The Carnival is generally held in the weeks preceding Lent, with the exact dates fluctuating from year to year. The city transforms into a playground of celebration and spectacle during this period. Venetians and tourists alike dress up in elaborate masks and costumes, entering a world of fantasy and masquerade.

The masks are possibly the most recognizable aspect of the Venice Carnival. They are a symbol of anonymity and independence, allowing participants to temporarily lose their identities and experience a sense of emancipation. There is a broad selection of masks to pick from, ranging from the basic white Bauta mask to

Copyrighted material

the delicately embellished Colombina, each with its own symbolism and history. Throughout the Carnival season, the city presents a slew of events and activities to keep visitors entertained. Grand masquerade balls are held in old palaces, where guests can dance the night away in opulent settings.

Street performances, live music, and parades with magnificent floats and costumed characters bring the streets and squares to life. Competitions for the best masks and costumes are also held, adding a friendly rivalry to the festivities.

The "Flight of the Angel" (Volo dell'Angelo), a stunning display that takes place in St. Mark's Square, is one of the highlights of the Venice Carnival.

Copyrighted material

During this ceremony, a costumed performer hung on a rope descends from the bell tower to the square. It is a dramatic event that marks the start of the Carnival celebrations and is received with great excitement and acclaim.

Exploring Venice during Carnival is a once-in-a-lifetime chance to immerse oneself in the city's rich cultural heritage. The breathtaking building, elaborate costumes, and vibrant atmosphere are a visual feast for the senses. Visitors can take a stroll along the canals, eat authentic Venetian food, and experience the city's lively energy as it comes alive with music, dance, and merriment.

Copyrighted material

The Venice Carnival is a season of enchantment and escapism when reality fades away to be replaced by a world of fiction. It embodies Venice's enduring charm by celebrating the spirit of creativity, individuality, and collective delight. Whether you want to dress up in a mask and fully participate or simply observe the activities, the Venice Carnival promises to be an exciting event that will leave you with memories to last a lifetime.

FESTA DEL REDENTORE: SPECTACULAR FIREWORKS

The Festa del Redentore, or Feast of the Redeemer, is one of Venice's most cherished and prominent cultural festivals. This yearly festival mixes religious observance with

Copyrighted material

lively festivities, bringing together inhabitants and visitors alike to remember the city's rescue from a horrific epidemic in the 16th century.

The Festa del Redentore dates back to 1576 when Venice was hit by a plague that killed thousands of its citizens. The Venetians swore to erect a church dedicated to the Redeemer in order to seek divine intervention, and if the city was spared further destruction, they would rejoice with an annual feast.

The disease gradually passed, and the magnificent Church of the Redentore was built on the island of Giudecca as a lasting memorial to this historic event.

Copyrighted material

The Festa del Redentore is held every year on the third Sunday of July. The spectacular religious procession, where a magnificent temporary bridge is created across the Giudecca Canal, connecting the Zattere promenade with the island of Giudecca, is the climax of the festivities.

The "Ponte del Redentore," as it is known, permits pilgrims to cross the lake and reach the Church of the Redentore for a solemn religious service.

Throughout the weekend, Venice comes alive with a vibrant environment. Buildings are adorned with colorful decorations, and boats of various sorts are dressed in festive clothing, creating a magnificent image on the canals.

Copyrighted material

Locals and visitors alike congregate in boats or on the shore to see stunning fireworks show over St. Mark's Basin. The fireworks are a spectacular display that draws large groups who eagerly await the hypnotic performance.

The Festa del Redentore is also a time for celebration and eating. Families and friends gather to share meals and sample traditional Venetian fare. It is a festive occasion in which the city's rich gastronomic legacy is commemorated alongside its religious significance.

Participating in the Festa del Redentore is a once-in-a-lifetime chance to immerse oneself in Venice's cultural traditions while also experiencing the city's feeling of camaraderie

Copyrighted material

and resilience. The event mixes religious devotion, history, and celebration to create a deeply meaningful and joyful environment. It is a chance to reflect on the city's history, pay homage to its customs, and celebrate the spirit of unity and hope that has endured over the ages.

STORICA REGATTA: HISTORIC BOAT RACE

The Regata Storica, or Historical Regatta, is a thrilling rowing event held each year in Venice, Italy. This historical event, which goes back to the 13th century, is deeply rooted in the city's nautical traditions and is one of the world's oldest and most famous rowing races.

Copyrighted material

The Regata Storica honors Venice's rich nautical heritage and the city's historical significance as a maritime power. The race is held on the first Sunday of September and includes a variety of rowing disciplines that demonstrate the participants' talent and athleticism.

Venetian rowing clubs, known as "remeri," battle fiercely against one another, each representing a different neighborhood and seeking victory.

The procession of historical boats that precedes the races is the highlight of the Regata Storica. As magnificently decorated boats glide along the city's canals, the procession is a mesmerizing spectacle that

Copyrighted material

transports onlookers back in time. From towering gondolas to elaborate 16th-century "bissone" boats used by nobles, each boat reflects a unique historical time or role.

The gondoliers and rowers are clothed in period costumes, which adds to the event's realism. The parade is accompanied by music and crowd cheers, creating a colorful and joyous environment along the canals.

Following the parade, the rowing races begin, with participants exhibiting their power and agility as they navigate the difficult course. The races are held on the Grand Canal, making for an exciting spectacle for fans who line the canal's banks to cheer on their favorite teams.

Copyrighted material

The Regata Storica is a celebration of Venetian culture and history as well as an athletic event. It provides tourists with a once-in-a-lifetime opportunity to observe the city's lasting nautical traditions while immersing themselves in the race's colorful atmosphere. With its rich tradition, civic spirit, and passion for rowing, the event encapsulates the heart of Venice.

Attending the Regata Storica allows you to experience Venice's ageless appeal while also witnessing the rowers' talent and tenacity as they navigate the historic waterways. It reflects the city's everlasting relationship with the sea and serves as a reminder of the importance of rowing in Venetian culture.

Copyrighted material

Whether you're a sports fan, a history buff, or simply looking for a memorable cultural experience, the Regata Storica provides an exciting and immersive view into Venice's heart and soul. It is a celebration of history, athleticism, and the tenacious spirit that has built this amazing city.

VENICE FILM FESTIVAL: GLAMOUR AND CINEMA

The Venice International Film Festival, often known as the Venice Film Festival, is one of the world's oldest and most famous film festivals. It is held every year in Venice, Italy, and features a broad range of foreign films ranging from art-house to popular blockbusters.

Copyrighted material

Since its inception in 1932, the festival has served as a prominent forum for filmmakers, performers, and industry professionals to present their work, participate in conversations, and celebrate the art of cinema.

The Venice Film Festival is held on Lido Island, which provides a gorgeous setting for the festival. The festival screens a wide selection of films in several categories over the course of 11 days, including the highly anticipated competition segment, when renowned awards such as the Golden Lion for Best Film are handed out.

Out of Competition, Orizzonti (Horizons), and Venice Classics, which focuses on the restoration of classic films, are also parts.

Copyrighted material

The festival gathers world-renowned filmmakers, actors, and industry insiders, resulting in a vibrant and dynamic atmosphere. Red carpet premieres, press conferences, and Q&As with directors add to the excitement by allowing fans to interact directly with the creative brains behind the films.

Aside from official screenings, the Venice Film Festival also sponsors parallel activities and initiatives that study many facets of cinema. These may include retrospectives, special screenings, workshops, and panel discussions, giving attendees a complete cinematic experience.

Copyrighted material

The Venice Film Festival is not just a venue for film screenings, but it also has a huge impact on the global cinema business. It has a history of discovering and promoting new talent, and many films that have premiered at the festival have gone on to garner critical recognition as well as commercial success.

The major honors and acclaim bestowed by the festival boost the fame of winning films and artists. The Golden Lion, given to the finest picture in the competition area, is one of the most coveted awards in the film industry, having helped begin the careers of many directors.

Attending the Venice Film Festival provides a once-in-a-lifetime opportunity to immerse

Copyrighted material

oneself in the enchantment of cinema in a dynamic and culturally diverse setting. It enables cinephiles, industry professionals, and cinema aficionados to discover new perspectives, participate in thought-provoking debates, and celebrate the power of narrative on the big screen.

Whether you are a film enthusiast, an aspiring filmmaker, or simply someone who appreciates the art of cinema, the Venice Film Festival offers a thrilling and immersive experience that exhibits the diversity and originality of the global film industry. It's a celebration of cinema's ability to capture, inspire, and challenge our worldviews.

Copyrighted material

CHAPTER 5

DAY TRIPS FROM VENICE

VERONA: ROMANCE AND SHAKESPEARE

Verona, in the Veneto region of northern Italy, is a city rich in history, culture, and romance. Verona, known around the world as the scene for Shakespeare's "Romeo and Juliet," enchants visitors with its attractive medieval alleyways, well-preserved old structures, and lively atmosphere.

The Arena di Verona, a spectacular Roman amphitheater dating from the first century AD, is one of the city's most recognizable sights.

Copyrighted material

It is now an open-air opera theater that hosts world-class performances during the annual Verona Opera Festival. The grandeur and acoustics of the Arena make a unique experience for opera and cultural aficionados alike.

The old core of Verona, a UNESCO World Heritage site, is a treasure trove of architectural marvels. The city's main square, Piazza delle Erbe, is a lively hub surrounded by colorful buildings, cafes, and the stunning Lamberti Tower. The nearby Porta Borsari, an ancient Roman gate, and the well-preserved Roman theater highlight Verona's rich past.

Copyrighted material

For admirers of Shakespeare's tragic love story, Casa di Giulietta, or Juliet's House, is a must-see. Visitors come to see Juliet's famous balcony and leave love notes on the walls. The setting exudes romance and a sense of eternal longing.

The gastronomic scene in Verona is a joy for foodies. Traditional delicacies available in the city include "Risotto all'Amarone," a savory rice dish cooked with Amarone wine, and "Pastissada de Caval," a slow-cooked horse meat stew that is a local delicacy. Verona is particularly famous for its pastries, including the "Pandoro," a golden Christmas cake, and the "Torta Russa," a tiered chocolate and almond cake.

Copyrighted material

Visitors will discover attractive squares, picturesque bridges, and secret corners that ooze the city's enchanting ambiance as they wander through Verona's narrow streets.

The Adige River flows elegantly through the city, providing spectacular views and a quiet setting for leisurely walks.

Verona is also a gateway to the picturesque Valpolicella wine area. A short drive from the city center will take you to rolling hills, vineyards, and wineries where you can sample world-famous wines like Amarone and Valpolicella.

Verona has a number of cultural events and festivals throughout the year, including the Verona Jazz Festival and the Verona Summer Drama Festival, which bring music, drama,

Copyrighted material

and art to the city's streets and ancient locations. Verona's timeless beauty, rich past, and romantic allure make it an enticing travel destination. Verona offers a magical experience that will leave you with lasting memories, whether you're strolling among old Roman ruins, experiencing the passion of an opera performance, or simply relishing the tastes of the region.

PADUA: HISTORIC UNIVERSITY TOWN

Padua, commonly known as Padova in Italian, is a charming city in northern Italy's Veneto region. Padua, with its almost 3,000-year history, is a treasure trove of

Copyrighted material

architectural marvels, cultural relics, and intellectual heritage.

The Scrovegni Chapel, one of the city's most popular attractions, is embellished with stunning frescoes by the legendary artist Giotto. The chapel's carefully conserved artwork shows biblical events and storylines, providing visitors with a glimpse into the 14th century's artistic excellence.

Padua is also known for its historic institution, the Institution of Padua, which was founded in 1222 and is one of the world's oldest universities. Throughout history, the institution has played an important role in developing intellectual and

Copyrighted material

scientific achievements by recruiting prominent professors and thinkers.

Padua's history as a center of learning has been enhanced by notable personalities such as Galileo Galilei and Nicolaus Copernicus.

The ancient heart of the city features exquisite squares, stately palaces, and winding streets that beg investigation.

The main plaza, Piazza delle Erbe, is a busy hub where locals and visitors congregate to enjoy outdoor cafes and appreciate the gorgeous architecture. The nearby Palazzo della Ragione, an enormous medieval palace, is a testimony to Padua's rich history.

Padua is also well-known for its religious sites. The Basilica of Saint Anthony, dedicated to the city's adored patron saint, is

Copyrighted material

a must-see pilgrimage destination. Inside the church, tourists can witness priceless works of art and pay their respects at Saint Anthony's tomb. The Orto Botanico di Padova, the world's oldest botanical garden, is a must-see for nature lovers.

Founded in 1545, the garden displays a diverse array of plants from throughout the world and provides a calm respite from the city's bustle. Padua, too, has its culinary wonders.

The city's food incorporates Veneto tastes, with dishes like "Bigoli," a thick pasta frequently served with a rich duck or rabbit sauce, and "Risotto alla Padovana," a creamy risotto made with local ingredients. Drink a glass of local wine with your dinner, such as

Copyrighted material

the famed white wine Soave or the red wine Colli Euganei.

Padua's robust artistic scene reflects its rich cultural past. The magnificent Teatro Verdi provides a range of acts, including opera, ballet, and concerts. Throughout the year, the city also holds a number of festivals and events that celebrate music, theater, and literature.

Padua's allure stems from its ability to perfectly integrate ancient heritage with modern energy. The intellectual legacy, architectural marvels, and cultural offers of the city combine to create a compelling atmosphere that beckons exploration and discovery.

Copyrighted material

Padua offers a rich and gratifying experience for travelers wishing to immerse themselves in the splendor of Italy's Veneto region, whether you appreciate rare art, delving into history, or simply relishing the local cuisine.

THE DOLOMITES: ALPINE BEAUTY

The Dolomites, a spectacular mountain range in northeastern Italy, fascinate travelers with its rough beauty, towering peaks, and breathtaking scenery. The Dolomites, a UNESCO World Heritage site, provide a wealth of outdoor adventures, scenic villages, and a unique cultural combination.

The Dolomites, known for their distinctive pale-colored rock formations, provide a breathtaking backdrop for sports such as

Copyrighted material

hiking, mountain biking, rock climbing, and skiing.

The mountains come alive in the summer with bright wildflowers, crystal-clear lakes, and winding pathways that lead to panoramic vistas. Exploring the Dolomites on foot allows you to get up close and personal with the magnificent alpine beauty while breathing in the pure mountain air.

The Dolomites are transformed into a winter sports paradise throughout the winter months. The region attracts skiers and snowboarders from all over the world due to its large network of ski resorts and well-groomed slopes.

There are alternatives for all levels of skill and experience, from mild slopes for

Copyrighted material

beginners to demanding terrain for specialists.

Cross-country skiing, snowshoeing, and ice climbing are among popular winter activities that allow tourists to immerse themselves in the winter splendor.

The Dolomites are not just a paradise for adventure lovers but also a cultural treasure trove. The region is filled with attractive Alpine villages and towns, each with its own distinct personality and customs.

Strolling through these charming towns, such as Cortina d'Ampezzo, Ortisei, and Bolzano, allows you to immerse yourself in the local way of life, admire classic architecture, and sample delectable regional cuisine. The Dolomites are also a cultural melting pot,

Copyrighted material

with influences from Italy, Austria, and Ladin.

With their distinct language and customs, the Ladin people bring a touch of cultural richness to the region. You can learn more about their legacy by visiting museums, festivals, and local traditions, which will give you a better grasp of the region's unique cultural tapestry.

Scenic drives through the Dolomites provide spectacular sights at every bend for those looking for a more relaxed experience. The Great Dolomites Road, also known as the Dolomites Highway, winds through some of the most breathtaking scenery, offering breathtaking views and numerous photo opportunities.

Copyrighted material

The Dolomites provide a genuinely immersive and unique experience with their natural beauty, outdoor activities, and cultural richness. The Dolomites beckon with their grandeur and charm, whether you're an adventurer, a nature lover, or someone seeking peace in a magnificent location. Discover the splendor of this majestic mountain range and make lifelong memories among the Dolomites' towering peaks and pure wildness.

TREVISO: PROSECCO AND CANALS

Treviso is a lovely city in northeastern Italy's Veneto region. Treviso, sometimes overshadowed by its more famous sister,

Copyrighted material

Venice, provides a pleasant respite for visitors seeking a more easygoing and authentic Italian experience.

The ancient heart of the city is a tangle of narrow alleyways, gorgeous canals, and medieval buildings that exude a timeless appeal. As you walk through the cobblestone streets, you'll come across gorgeous piazzas like Piazza dei Signori and Piazza Rinaldi, where locals meet to mingle and drink coffee or prosecco.

Treviso is famous for its well-preserved city walls that ring the historic core and offer an insight into the city's rich history. Walking around the defensive walls provides panoramic views of the city and its surrounding flora, resulting in a tranquil and

Copyrighted material

romantic mood. The Sile River, which runs through Treviso, is one of the city's features. You may experience the city's natural beauty and calm environment by strolling along its banks or taking a boat trip. The river also has a rich ecosystem, making it a sanctuary for birdwatchers and wildlife lovers.

The majestic Treviso Cathedral, a Romanesque and Gothic masterpiece filled with exquisite sculptures and stunning murals, is one of the city's architectural gems. Another must-see monument is the Palazzo dei Trecento, a medieval palace that served as the seat of government and provides insight into Treviso's political and cultural history.

Copyrighted material

Treviso is well-known for its food and wine. The region is well-known for its superb Prosecco wine, and wine tastings and vineyard tours are available in the surrounding countryside. Traditional foods served in the city's trattorias and osterias include "Risotto al Radicchio," a savory risotto prepared with local red chicory, and "Tiramisu," a wonderful dessert that originated in the region.

Local markets, such as the old fish market in Piazza San Parisio, provide a sensory overload. You can immerse yourself in the lively sensations of the Veneto area by sampling fresh local fruit, regional cheeses, and a range of cured meats.

Copyrighted material

Throughout the year, Treviso offers a variety of cultural events, such as art exhibitions, music festivals, and theater performances. The dynamic cultural landscape of the city offers possibilities to engage with local customs and immerse yourself in the colorful atmosphere.

Treviso provides a lovely and authentic Italian experience with its tranquil canals, historic charm, and gastronomic pleasures. Treviso encourages you to discover its hidden gems and embrace the art of dolce far niente - the sweetness of doing nothing - whether you're meandering through its enchanting alleyways, eating local specialties, or simply enjoying the laid-back ambiance.

Copyrighted material

CHAPTER 6

PRACTICAL TIPS FOR YOUR STAY

DINING AND SHOPPING SUGGESTIONS

Dining and shopping in Venice provide a rich tapestry of gastronomic pleasures as well as one-of-a-kind stores. Here are some ideas to make your visit more enjoyable:

DINING

Ristorante Da Ivo: This popular restaurant near St. Mark's Square offers a typical Venetian dining experience with a concentration on seafood delicacies. While

Copyrighted material

enjoying the friendly ambiance, indulge in meals such as spaghetti alle vongole (clams) or risotto al nero di seppia (squid ink risotto).

<u>Osteria Alle Testiere</u>: Known for its superb seafood dishes and fresh ingredients acquired from the Rialto Market, this tiny osteria is a must-visit.

With a limited number of tables, book a reservation in advance to savor their delectable delicacies.

<u>Trattoria Antiche Carampane</u>: This quaint trattoria, tucked away in a quiet corner, serves typical Venetian cuisine in a comfortable atmosphere. For a true taste of the city, try sarde in saor (sweet and sour sardines) and fegato alla veneziana (Venetian-style liver).

Copyrighted material

SHOPPING

<u>Rialto Market</u>: Located near the Rialto Bridge, this lively market is a foodie's paradise. Visit the lively kiosks selling fresh produce, local fish, cheeses, and spices. It's ideal for picking up picnic items or sampling Venetian specialties.

<u>Calle Larga XXII Marzo</u>: This lovely street is lined with upscale retailers and designer shops. Enjoy some shopping therapy as you stroll down this stylish boulevard, which features everything from luxury apparel companies to fine jewelry and accessories.

<u>Fondaco dei Tedeschi</u>: Near the Rialto Bridge, this antique building has been turned into a luxury retail center.

Copyrighted material

Explore its multi-level department store, which features a diverse selection of clothing, accessories, cosmetics, and home items.

Don't miss out on the rooftop patio, which offers panoramic views of Venice.

<u>Murano Glass</u>: Take a vaporetto to Murano, an island noted for its magnificent glassware. Explore the glass factories and stores, where you may marvel at the exquisite glassblowing processes and buy one-of-a-kind handcrafted items as souvenirs or gifts.

<u>Cannaregio District</u>: Venture outside of the main tourist attractions to explore handmade shops and local retailers. You'll find a variety of one-of-a-kind items, including handmade leather goods, distinctive Venetian masks, and traditional crafts.

Copyrighted material

Remember to explore the city's lesser-known streets and squares since they frequently hold hidden jewels just waiting to be discovered.

Venice's dining and shopping scenes offer a unique blend of heritage and modern flair, ensuring that every visitor has a distinctive and gratifying experience.

HOW TO USE THE VAPORETTO & WATER TAXI SYSTEM

Navigating Venice's vaporetto and water taxi systems may appear intimidating at first, but with a little help, you'll find it to be an efficient and pleasurable way to explore the city's unique waterways.

Copyrighted material

Here are some hints for navigating the vaporetto and water taxi systems:

VAPORETTO

<u>Understanding the Lines</u>: The vaporetto is Venice's public water bus system, and it operates on a number of lines that are labeled with numbers and letters. Examine the vaporetto map or navigation software to find the lines that will take you to your intended destinations.

Tickets and passes must be purchased before boarding the vaporetto. They are available for purchase at ticket booths, authorized resellers, and automated ticket machines at key vaporetto stops. If you want to ride the vaporetto regularly during your visit, consider purchasing a travel card or a day

Copyrighted material

pass. Wait at the designated vaporetto stop and be prepared to queue, especially during peak hours. Allow people to depart before boarding the vaporetto. Take note of the line number displayed on the vaporetto to verify you're on the correct one.

<u>Vaporetto Etiquette:</u> Once on board, go to the center to make room for other passengers. Priority should be given to elderly, disabled, or pregnant passengers if seats are available. Keep your stuff out of the aisles and be considerate of other passengers.

TAXI ON THE WATER

Water Taxi Services: Water taxis are private boats that provide a more elegant and personalized mode of transportation around Venice.

Copyrighted material

They can be summoned at approved water taxi stands or pre-booked through a service provider. Water taxi prices are normally arranged with the driver prior to the ride. Expect to pay more than if you took the vaporetto. Before boarding the water taxi, discuss the rate and any additional charges, such as luggage or late-night penalties.

Private Water Taxi Services: Several firms offer pre-booked private water taxi services if you like. You can schedule the service ahead of time and choose your pick-up and drop-off locations. Private water taxis are more convenient and private than public transportation, but they are more expensive.

Copyrighted material

GENERAL ADVICE

Examine the Timetable: Keep an eye on the vaporetto and water taxi schedules, especially if you're traveling late at night. During some times, services may operate with a reduced frequency.

Validate Your Ticket: Before boarding, remember to validate your vaporetto ticket at the ticket validation machines situated at the vaporetto stops. If you are detected without a valid ticket during ticket inspections, you may be fined.

Consider Luggage: If you have heavy or cumbersome luggage, consider using the luggage storage containers on the vaporetto. Because water taxis may have limited space,

Copyrighted material

advise the driver about the size of your cargo when negotiating the fee.

<u>Stay Informed:</u> Keep an eye out for any modifications or updates to the vaporetto and water taxi schedules since they may vary due to weather or special events.

By being acquainted with Venice's vaporetto and water taxi systems, you will be able to navigate the city's waterways with ease, making your exploration of this unique and wonderful location even more unforgettable.

ADVICE ON SAFETY AND SECURITY

It is critical to consider safety and security when visiting any destination, especially Venice. Here are some common safety precautions to take when in Venice:

Copyrighted material

<u>Be Wary of Pickpockets</u>: As with any major tourist location, pickpocketing can occur in busy areas. Always keep an eye on your belongings, especially in popular tourist areas, public transportation, and crowded markets. To carry your valuables, choose a lockable bag or pocketbook and consider a money belt or hidden pouch.

<u>Stay in Well-Lit and populous locations</u>: When walking around at night, stay in Well-Lit and populous locations. Avoid secluded streets or alleyways, especially if you're not familiar with them.

<u>Be Wary of Public</u> Transit: Be wary of public transit, such as vaporettos or buses. Keep an eye on your possessions and be aware of your surroundings.

Copyrighted material

If you're traveling late at night, it's best to sit near other passengers or near the driver.

Beware of Scams: Be aware of anyone who approaches you with an offer or a request for money. When dealing with street vendors, use caution and be cautious of classic tourist frauds such as false petitions, unwanted help, or diversion techniques.

Follow Local Laws and Customs: Learn about the laws and customs of Venice and Italy in general. Respect cultural conventions, dress accordingly, and be aware of local prohibitions, such as those prohibiting feeding pigeons or swimming in canals.

Make a list of vital emergency numbers, such as the local police, ambulance, and fire service.

Copyrighted material

The emergency number in Italy is 112. Keep a copy of your passport and other key documents apart from the originals in a safe place.

Travel Insurance: Having travel insurance that covers medical expenditures, trip cancellation, and lost or stolen possessions is always a good idea. Examine your insurance policy to confirm that it covers your vacation to Venice.

Keep Up to Date: Keep up to date on any travel advisories or safety information released by your country's government or relevant agencies. When you arrive in Venice, you need to register with your embassy or consulate.

Copyrighted material

You may assist in ensuring a safe and happy vacation to Venice by following these safety precautions and exercising common sense.

Trust your instincts, be alert of your surroundings, and take the necessary precautions to keep yourself and your things safe during your visit.

TRAVELERS BASIC LANGUAGE GUIDE

A rudimentary familiarity with the local language will substantially enhance your experience when visiting Venice. Here's a language guide with some key Italian phrases and terminology to help you communicate while on vacation:

Greetings and Basic Expressions:

Copyrighted material

Buongiorno: Good morning / Good day

Buonasera: Good evening

Ciao: Hello / Goodbye (informal)

Grazie: Thank you

Prego: You're welcome / Please (in response to "grazie")

Scusa / Scusami: Excuse me / Sorry (informal)

Mi scusi: Excuse me / I'm sorry (formal)

Per favore: Please

Sì: Yes

No: No

Getting Around

Dov'è...? / Dov'è la stazione? - Where is...? / Where is the train station?

Quanto costa? - How much does it cost?

Copyrighted material

Vorrei un biglietto per... - I would like a ticket to...

A che ora parte il treno / vaporetto? - What time does the train / vaporetto leave?

Destinazione - Destination

Partenza - Departure

Arrivo - Arrival

Eating and Ordering:

Un tavolo per uno / due, per favore - A table for one / two, please

Il menù, per favore - The menu, please

Vorrei... - I would like...

Un caffè / un cappuccino - A coffee / a cappuccino

Un bicchiere di vino rosso / bianco - A glass of red / white wine

Il conto, per favore - The bill, please

Copyrighted material

Shopping:

Quanto costa? - How much does it cost?

Posso provarlo? - Can I try it on?

Cerco... - I'm looking for...

Non-capisco - I don't understand

Mi piace / Non mi piace - I like it / I don't like it

Accettate carte di credito? - Do you accept credit cards?

Emergencies

Aiuto! - Help!

Ho bisogno di un dottore - I need a doctor

Ho perso il mio passaporto - I lost my passport

Ho bisogno di assistenza - I need assistance

Numbers:

1: uno

Copyrighted material

2: due

3: tre

4: quattro

5: cinque

6: sei

7: sette

8: otto

9: nove

10: dieci

Remember that Italians love it when foreigners try to speak their language, even if it's only a few simple phrases. Use these expressions freely, and be patient and polite when conversing. The majority of Venetians speak English and will gladly assist you. Have a wonderful vacation in Venice, and have a safe journey!

Copyrighted material

TIPS & RECOMMENDATIONS

As you plan your vacation to Venice, consider the following last advice and recommendations to ensure a pleasant and unforgettable experience:

Plan and book ahead of time: Venice is a popular tourist destination, especially during high seasons. To guarantee the finest alternatives and minimize disappointment, it is important to plan and reserve hotels, activities, and transportation in advance.

Get Lost in Venice's alleys: While having a general sense of direction is crucial, don't be afraid to get lost in Venice's fascinating maze of alleys and canals. Walking about the city can bring you to hidden jewels and surprising discoveries.

Copyrighted material

Respect the City and Its citizens: Venice is a live, breathing city with citizens, not merely a tourist attraction. Respect their way of life, observe local customs, and keep noise levels in mind, especially in residential areas.

Dress Comfortably and Respectfully: Because Venice's streets and pathways are mostly cobblestones, wear comfortable walking shoes. Dress modestly and cover your shoulders and knees when visiting churches or other religious institutions.

Use Public Transportation Wisely: While the vaporetto system is a convenient method to navigate the city's canals, if you prefer to stroll, keep in mind that Venice is rather small. Consider getting a travel card for

Copyrighted material

unlimited vaporetto trips throughout your stay.

Enjoy typical Venetian meals such as cicchetti (small tapas-style plates), sarde in saor (marinated sardines), risotto, and local seafood. Don't pass up the chance to sample a gelato or an espresso at one of the charming cafés.

Capture the Magic: Venice is a photographer's dream, so bring your camera or smartphone to capture the city's enchantment. Early morning and late evening are especially beautiful times to capture breathtaking sights while avoiding crowds.

Copyrighted material

<u>Be Aware of the Environmental Impact</u>: Overtourism and the impact of high numbers of visitors pose issues for Venice.

Be mindful of your actions and strive to reduce waste, protect the environment, and promote sustainable tourism practices.

<u>Take time to rest</u>: Amid the bustling streets and crowded sights, take time to rest and experience Venice's peaceful side. To absorb the atmosphere, sit along the canals, take a gondola ride, or find a peaceful corner in one of the city's gorgeous squares.

<u>Embrace serendipity:</u> Venice is a city full of surprises and happy accidents. Allow yourself to be open to new experiences, serendipitous meetings, and the distinctive atmosphere that makes Venice so remarkable.

Copyrighted material

You're ready to go on your Venice journey now that you've read these bits of advice and recommendations. Accept the city's allure, immerse yourself in its rich history and culture, and make memories to last a lifetime. Good luck on your journey!

Copyrighted material

CONCLUSION

Venice is a mesmerizing city that provides visitors with a one-of-a-kind and unforgettable experience. Venice has something for everyone, from its gorgeous canals and historic buildings to its rich culture and delectable cuisine.

You may completely immerse yourself in the Venetian way of life by digging into the city's history, discovering its neighborhoods, and participating in its exciting festivals. Venice will leave you with lasting memories, whether you're meandering through St. Mark's Square, admiring the art treasures at Gallerie dell'Accademia, or tasting real Italian meals in local trattorias.

Copyrighted material

It is critical to plan your trip ahead of time, taking into account the optimal time to visit, visa requirements, lodging possibilities, and transportation options. Respecting local norms and making an attempt to converse in Italian can enrich your experience and help you connect with the city and its people.

Take time to absorb Venice's distinctive beauty, exquisite architecture, and wonderful ambiance as you travel the streets, canals, and bridges. Whether you're photographing beautiful views or simply relaxing in the city's tranquility, Venice has a way of winning the hearts of its tourists.

Don't forget to cherish the moments, embrace the unexpected, and depart with a sense of awe and gratitude for the lovely city of

Copyrighted material

Venice as you bid farewell to this floating metropolis.

City of Venice at sunset

Copyrighted material

APPRECIATORY MESSAGE

Dear Esteemed Customers,

We would like to express our heartfelt gratitude for choosing our book and entrusting us with your time. Your unwavering support and insightful feedback are much appreciated.

We sincerely appreciate your aid in submitting an honest review as we continually endeavor to improve our work and produce impactful information.

Your reviews are extremely valuable not just to us as authors, but also to prospective readers looking for information. We sincerely respect your views and comments, whether you felt our book was amazing or believe there were flaws. Your feedback is an ongoing source of

Copyrighted material

inspiration for us to develop stories that are truly meaningful to you. We would appreciate it if you could take a few moments to leave a review on Amazon, as your words have the potential to dramatically impact the success and reach of our book, allowing it to reach a bigger audience.

Remember that your review does not have to be long or complicated. Simply giving your honest thoughts, emphasizing aspects that are related to you, or underlining notable components would be quite beneficial.

We want to thank you again for being a part of our journey as authors. We value your ongoing support and participation tremendously. We look forward to reading your evaluations and growing alongside you.

Best regards,

Printed in Great Britain
by Amazon

27988667R00086